S0-AFA-943

Very special thanks to Robin Jones Gunn
for her help in making Tupsu a reality.

To my wife and daughters
with love, Alexander

To my animal-loving niece, Milo Rebecca
with love, Melody

TUPSU
published by Gold'n'Honey Books, *a part of the Questar publishing family*
Text © 1997 by Questar Publishers
Illustrations © 1997 by Alexander Reichstein,
Design by Kevin Keller

International Standard Book Number: 1-57673-052-2
Printed in Mexico

Scripture taken from the *New King James Version*
© 1979, 1980, 1982 by Thomas Nelson, Inc. Used by permission. All rights reserved.

ALL RIGHTS RESERVED
No part of this publication may be reproduced, stored in a retrieval system, or transmitted, in any form
or by any means— electronic, mechanical, photocopying, recording, or otherwise—without prior written permission.
For information: QUESTAR PUBLISHERS, INC. - PO BOX 1720 - SISTERS, OREGON 97759

Library of Congress Cataloging-in-Publication Data
Carlson, Melody.
Tupsu, the squirrel who was afraid / by Melody Carlson; illustrations by
Alexander Reichstein.
p.   cm.
Summary: Tupsu the squirrel learns a lesson about what it means to
trust God instead of being afraid.
ISBN 1-57673-052-2 (alk. paper)
[1. Squirrels—Fiction. 2. Fear—Fiction. 3. Christian life—Fiction.]
I. Reichstein, Alexander, ill. II. Title.
PZ7.C216637Tu   1997
[E]—dc21
                                                    96-49451
                                                    CIP
                                                    AC

97   98   99   00   01   02   03 — 10   9   8   7   6   5   4   3   2   1

TUPSU The Squirrel Who was Afraid

Melody Carlson illustrated by Alexander Reichstein

Deep in the Great Forest lives a squirrel named Tupsu. There has never been a more carefree creature! He likes to scamper across the brook — it feels just like flying.

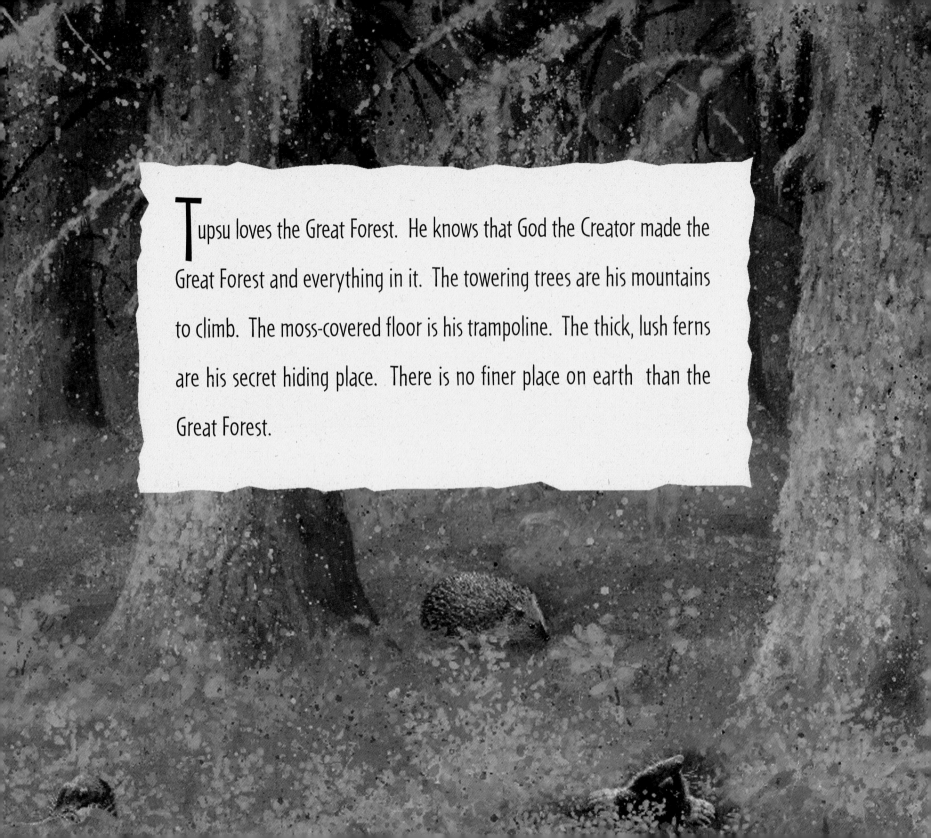

Tupsu loves the Great Forest. He knows that God the Creator made the Great Forest and everything in it. The towering trees are his mountains to climb. The moss-covered floor is his trampoline. The thick, lush ferns are his secret hiding place. There is no finer place on earth than the Great Forest.

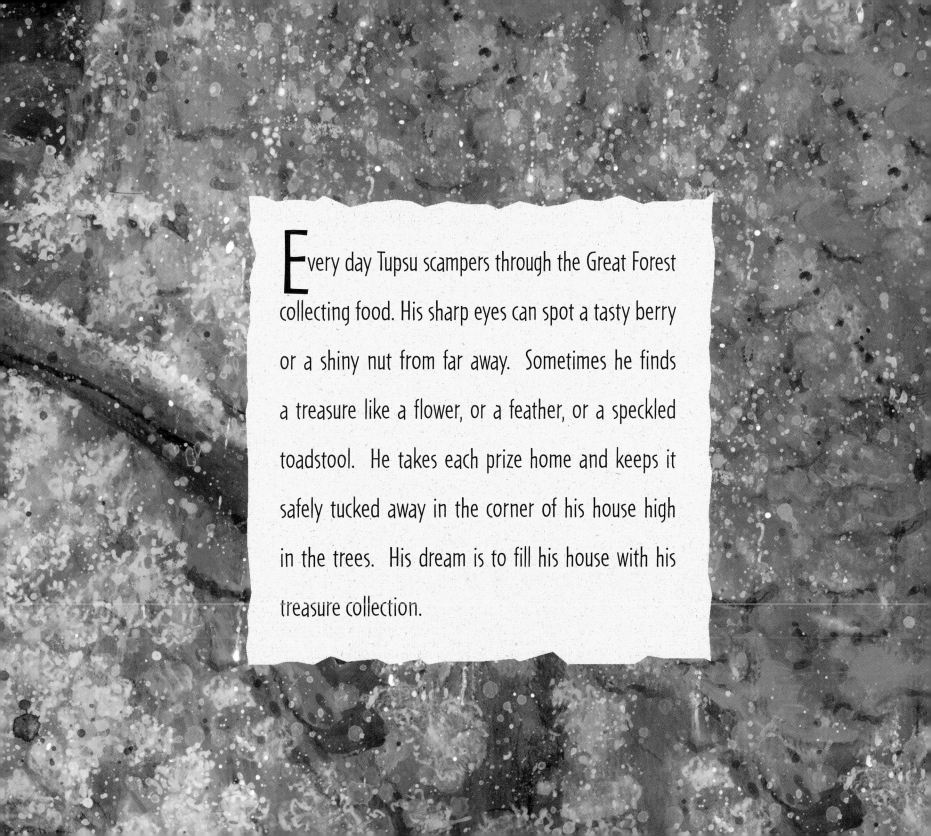

Every day Tupsu scampers through the Great Forest collecting food. His sharp eyes can spot a tasty berry or a shiny nut from far away. Sometimes he finds a treasure like a flower, or a feather, or a speckled toadstool. He takes each prize home and keeps it safely tucked away in the corner of his house high in the trees. His dream is to fill his house with his treasure collection.

At night Tupsu loves to watch the stars blink through the treetops. They remind him of his treasures. He wonders if perhaps the stars are part of God the Creator's treasure collection. With a happy sigh, Tupsu snuggles down and falls asleep, listening to the wind singing in the treetops.

Each morning Tupsu wakes to the sound of the birds chirping and singing. Their happy song tells him it's time to climb down from his home so he can collect food and, hopefully, a few new treasures.

On one fine morning, Tupsu awoke and began singing along with the birds. Then something terrible happened.

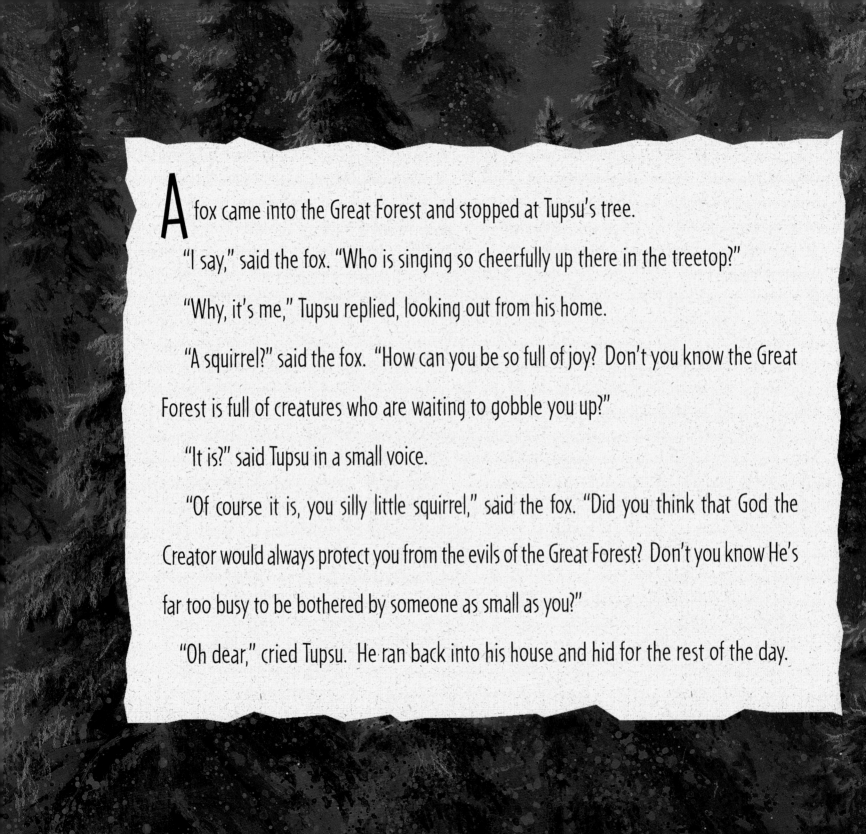

A fox came into the Great Forest and stopped at Tupsu's tree.

"I say," said the fox. "Who is singing so cheerfully up there in the treetop?"

"Why, it's me," Tupsu replied, looking out from his home.

"A squirrel?" said the fox. "How can you be so full of joy? Don't you know the Great Forest is full of creatures who are waiting to gobble you up?"

"It is?" said Tupsu in a small voice.

"Of course it is, you silly little squirrel," said the fox. "Did you think that God the Creator would always protect you from the evils of the Great Forest? Don't you know He's far too busy to be bothered by someone as small as you?"

"Oh dear," cried Tupsu. He ran back into his house and hid for the rest of the day.

The next morning, Tupsu knew he must go on his daily hunt for food. But he was still frightened by what the fox had said. Carefully and quietly, Tupsu climbed down from his tree and scampered just as fast as he could across the brook in search for food.

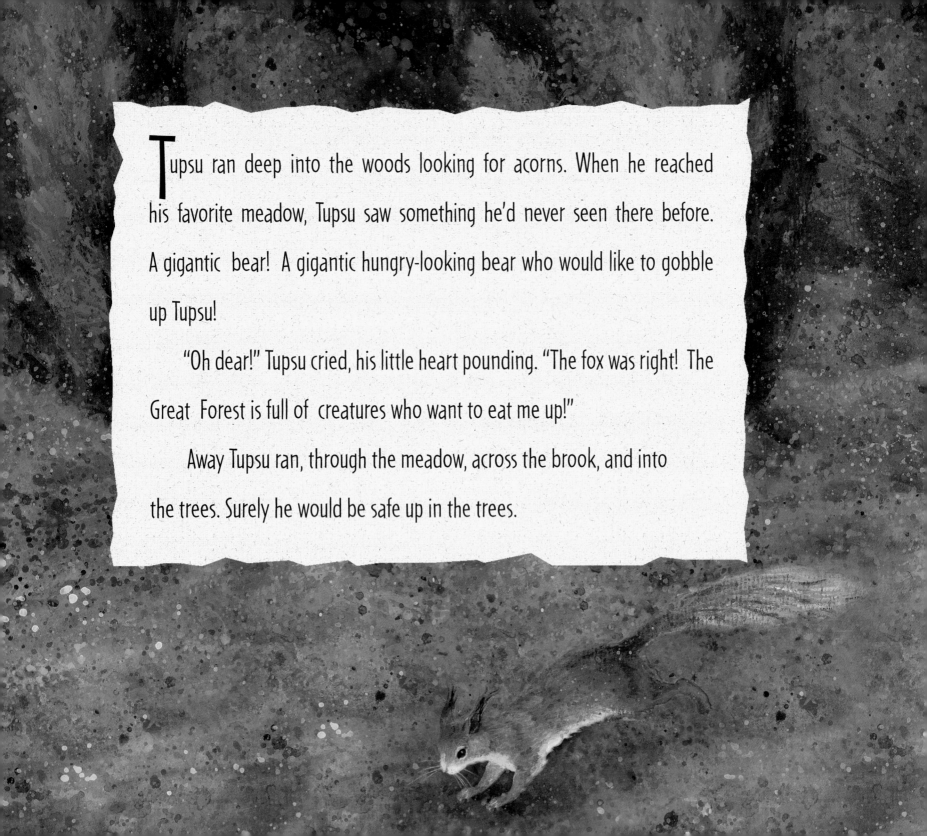

Tupsu ran deep into the woods looking for acorns. When he reached his favorite meadow, Tupsu saw something he'd never seen there before. A gigantic bear! A gigantic hungry-looking bear who would like to gobble up Tupsu!

"Oh dear!" Tupsu cried, his little heart pounding. "The fox was right! The Great Forest is full of creatures who want to eat me up!"

Away Tupsu ran, through the meadow, across the brook, and into the trees. Surely he would be safe up in the trees.

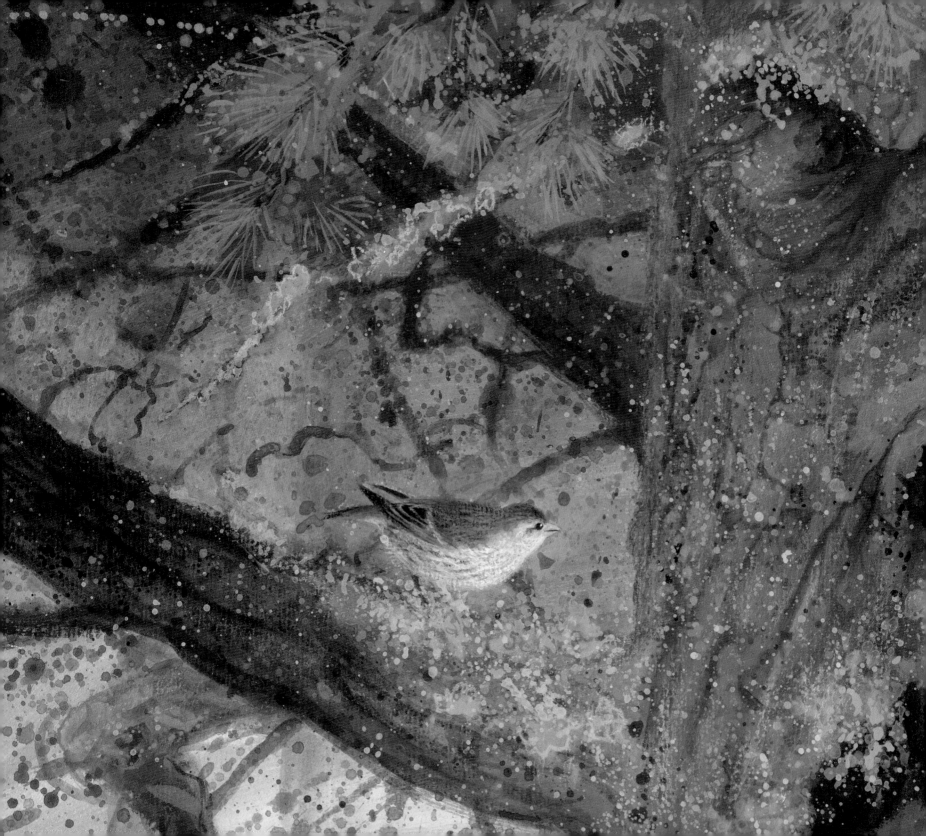

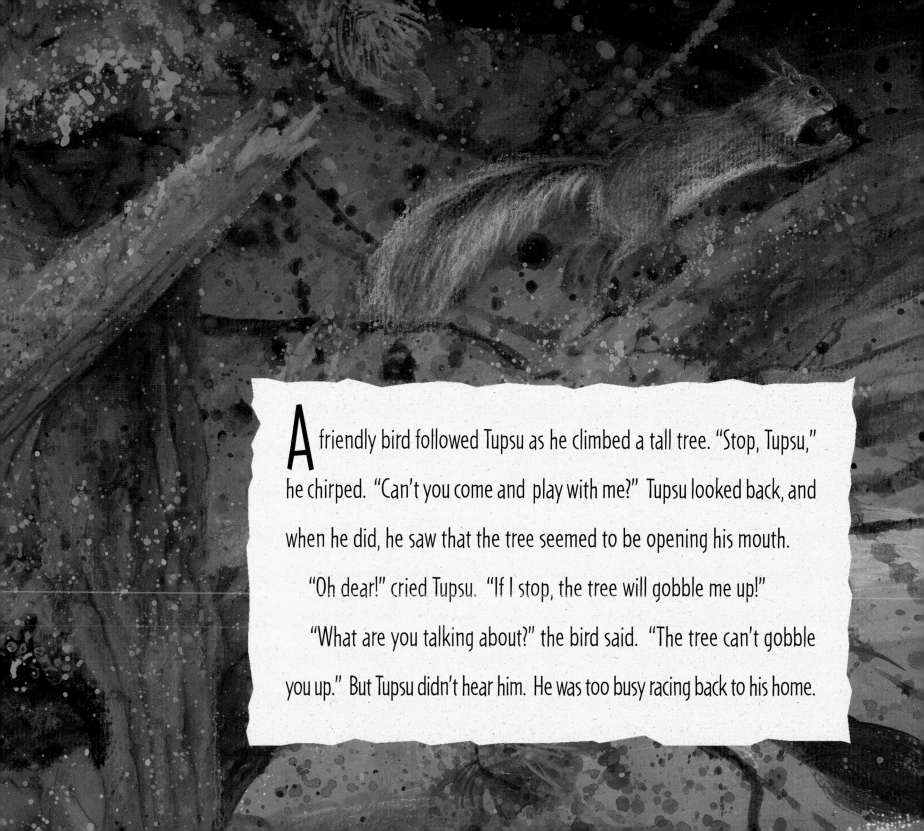

A friendly bird followed Tupsu as he climbed a tall tree. "Stop, Tupsu," he chirped. "Can't you come and play with me?" Tupsu looked back, and when he did, he saw that the tree seemed to be opening his mouth.

"Oh dear!" cried Tupsu. "If I stop, the tree will gobble me up!"

"What are you talking about?" the bird said. "The tree can't gobble you up." But Tupsu didn't hear him. He was too busy racing back to his home.

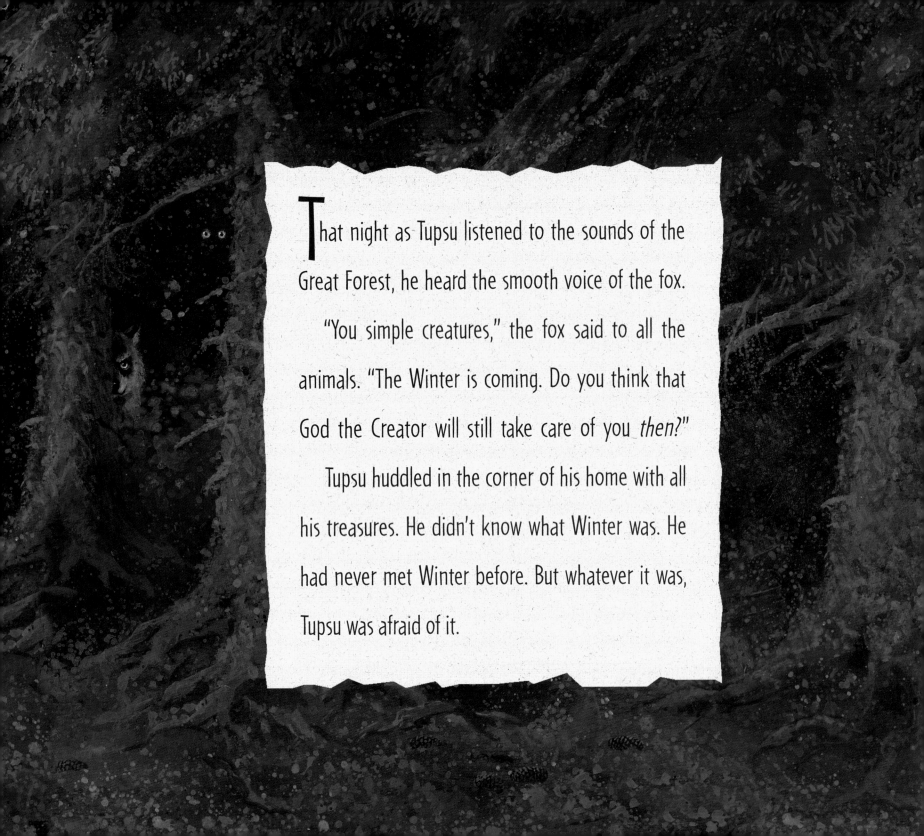

That night as Tupsu listened to the sounds of the Great Forest, he heard the smooth voice of the fox.

"You simple creatures," the fox said to all the animals. "The Winter is coming. Do you think that God the Creator will still take care of you *then?*"

Tupsu huddled in the corner of his home with all his treasures. He didn't know what Winter was. He had never met Winter before. But whatever it was, Tupsu was afraid of it.

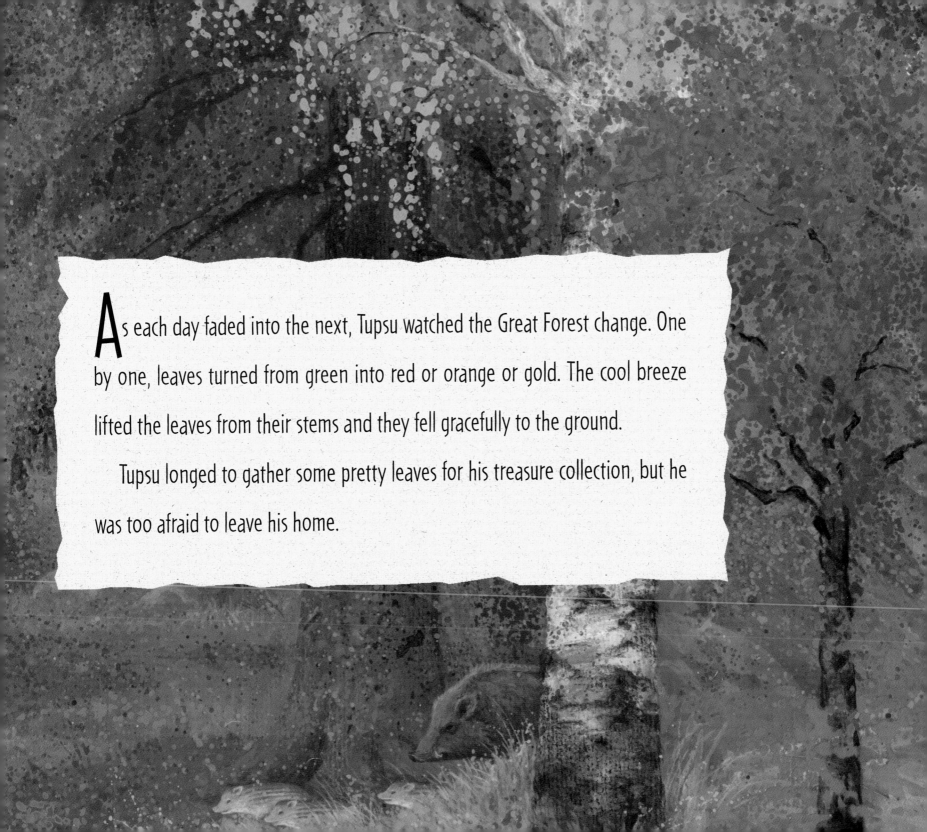

As each day faded into the next, Tupsu watched the Great Forest change. One by one, leaves turned from green into red or orange or gold. The cool breeze lifted the leaves from their stems and they fell gracefully to the ground.

Tupsu longed to gather some pretty leaves for his treasure collection, but he was too afraid to leave his home.

Then Winter came. Tupsu knew it was Winter, for the Great Forest was silent now. Silent and cold. Tupsu watched as lacy white flakes drifted down from the sky, covering all the leaves.

He wondered if the fox was right. Had God the Creator forgotten all of His creatures?

Tupsu became more and more curious about changes in the Great Forest. What would it be like to scamper in all that white snow? Finally, he just had to know!

Down he went, landing in the snow with a big plop. The snow felt cold on his little feet. His quick eyes darted right and left as he scampered. He was on the lookout for frightening creatures.

When Tupsu came to the brook he stopped. His heart began to pound fiercely. Even the brook now had a scary face! With a swish of his tail, Tupsu fled.

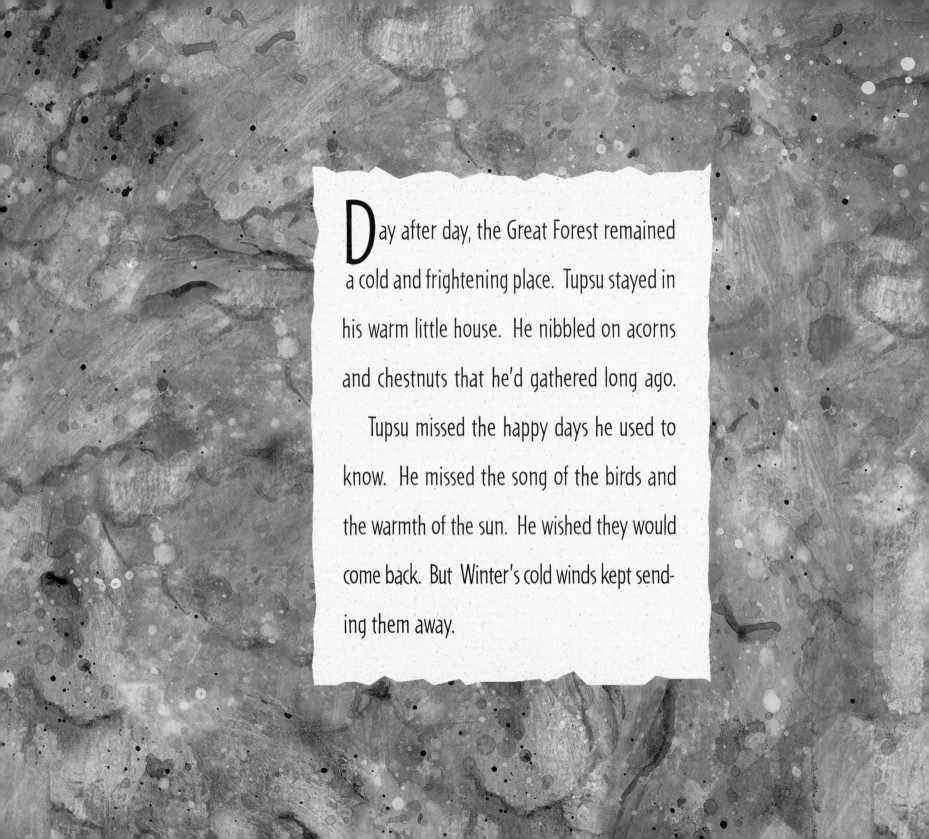

Day after day, the Great Forest remained a cold and frightening place. Tupsu stayed in his warm little house. He nibbled on acorns and chestnuts that he'd gathered long ago.

Tupsu missed the happy days he used to know. He missed the song of the birds and the warmth of the sun. He wished they would come back. But Winter's cold winds kept sending them away.

Little by little, the cold snow began to melt. The afternoons felt warmer and a few birds started to sing. The Great Forest began to look the way it used to when Tupsu was free to scamper about. But Tupsu was still afraid. The Great Forest was still full of terrible creatures just as the fox had said. Tupsu had seen the angry bear in the meadow. He knew the old tree had a wide-open mouth, ready to gobble him up. Even the brook frightened Tupsu.

Then one day, he heard a voice call out, "Hello! Are you Tupsu?"

"Yes, I am." Tupsu timidly peeked out of his home. "Who are you?"

"I'm Kirreli. The old moose said I might find a new friend here. Will you come play with me?"

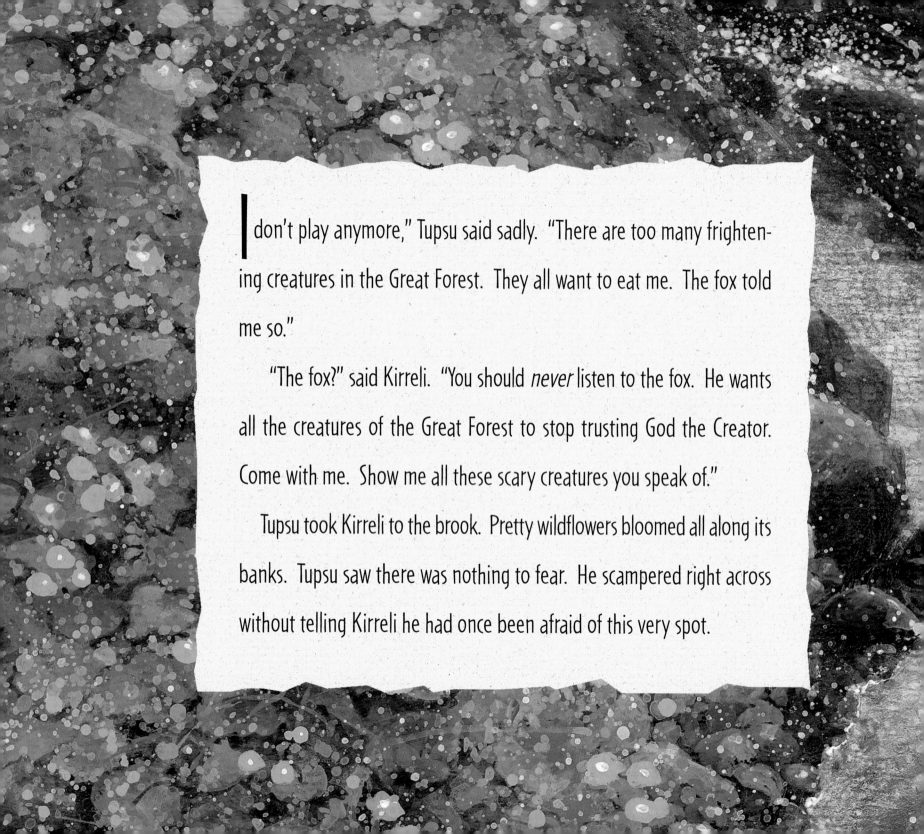

I don't play anymore," Tupsu said sadly. "There are too many frightening creatures in the Great Forest. They all want to eat me. The fox told me so."

"The fox?" said Kirreli. "You should *never* listen to the fox. He wants all the creatures of the Great Forest to stop trusting God the Creator. Come with me. Show me all these scary creatures you speak of."

Tupsu took Kirreli to the brook. Pretty wildflowers bloomed all along its banks. Tupsu saw there was nothing to fear. He scampered right across without telling Kirreli he had once been afraid of this very spot.

This way," said Tupsu. Kirreli followed Tupsu deep into the Great Forest. Tupsu stopped short.
The scary tree with the big mouth had toppled over and there was no mouth to be seen at all.

   "Come on," Tupsu said. "I know the bear is real. I only hope he doesn't eat both of us in one
big bite!" Off they scampered to the edge of the meadow where Tupsu was sure they'd find the
gigantic bear.

Is this your gigantic bear?" Kirreli asked when they got to the edge of the Great Forest.

"Oh dear," said Tupsu. "All this time I have been afraid of a rock."

"Well, it is a very large rock," said Kirreli.

"But it's only a rock," said Tupsu. "And I was afraid because I listened to the fox. He made me think that God the Creator was too busy to take care of me since I am only a little squirrel."

They were quiet for a moment. Tupsu listened to all the wonderful sounds in the Great Forest.

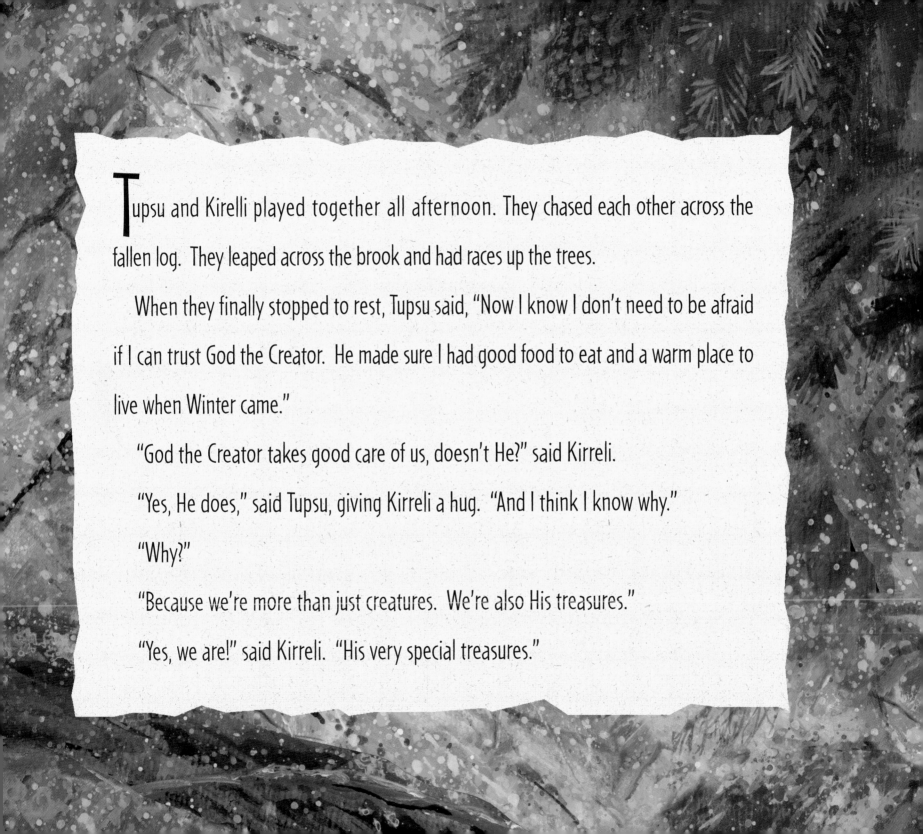

Tupsu and Kirelli played together all afternoon. They chased each other across the fallen log. They leaped across the brook and had races up the trees.

When they finally stopped to rest, Tupsu said, "Now I know I don't need to be afraid if I can trust God the Creator. He made sure I had good food to eat and a warm place to live when Winter came."

"God the Creator takes good care of us, doesn't He?" said Kirreli.

"Yes, He does," said Tupsu, giving Kirreli a hug. "And I think I know why."

"Why?"

"Because we're more than just creatures. We're also His treasures."

"Yes, we are!" said Kirreli. "His very special treasures."

There is no fear in love; but perfect love casts out fear...

The one who fears has not been made perfect in love.

1 John 4:18 (NKJV)